The gin-clear waters of the Caribbean Sea contain some of the world's most interesting and beautiful underwater scenery. Warm and unpolluted, the Caribbean waters enhance the growth of hard-coral reefs. The reefs, in turn, are populated by great multitudes of marine organisms. As a result, there is excellent diving around most Caribbean islands, and the Caribbean has become a scuba diver's mecca.

In the waters surrounding the Cayman Islands the diving is superb. The structure of the reefs offers infinite variety. The abundance and diversity of the marine life is amazing—after making well over 3,000 dives in these waters, I am still finding exciting new creatures that I have never seen before. I have lived and dived in the Caymans for more than six years—a memorable and richly rewarding experience. It is my hope that this book, in some small way, relates my experiences, and my impressions of this underwater wonderland.

Paul Humann

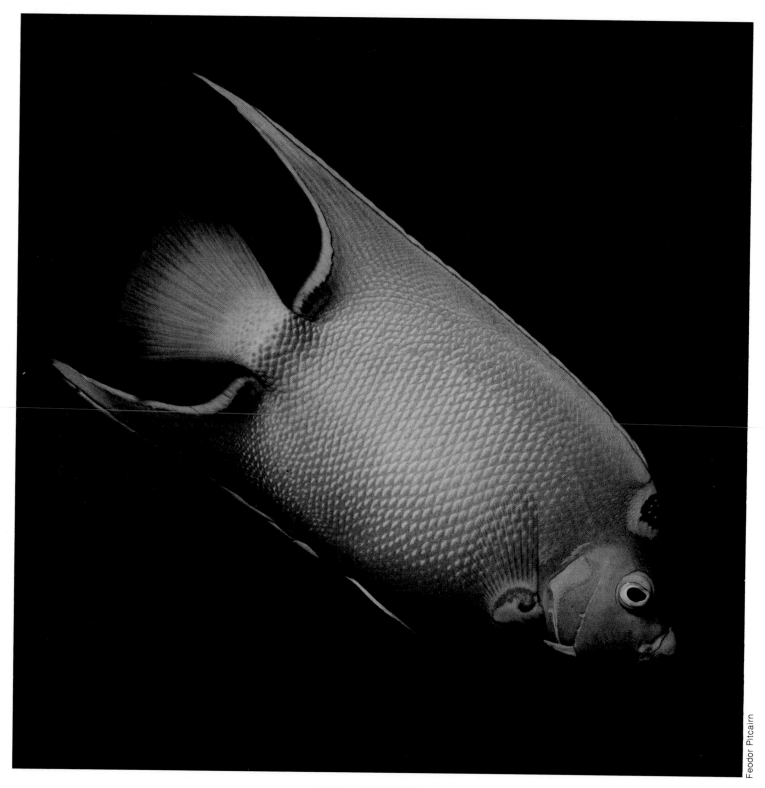

QUEEN ANGELFISH

To Dick —
Hope this book will help
you understand more of what
you see while in the water.
Best wishes,
Paul Humann

Cayman
Underwater Paradise

By Paul Humann and Feodor Pitcairn
Text by Paul Humann

Reef Dwellers Press

We are most grateful to those
who have generously given of
their time and knowledge to
help with the identification
of the marine life.

Sponges:
Dr. Henry M. Reiswig of McGill University, Montreal
Gorgonians:
Dr. Timothy O'Brien of The University of Illinois at Urbana
Fish:
Dr. James E. Böhlke of The Academy of Natural Sciences, Philadelphia

Edited by Kirstin Pitcairn

Charts by Douglas Reed
Printed by Consolidated/Drake Press

Libr. Congress #79-84293
ISBN #0-9602530-0-9 First Edition

Published by—Reef Dwellers Press
                Bryn Athyn, Pa. 19009

Contents

SEVEN MILE BEACH

The Islands

The Caymans are three small islands in the placid, clear blue waters of the northwest Caribbean Sea. Cayman Brac and Little Cayman are only a few miles apart, separated from Grand Cayman by almost 70 miles of ocean. Cayman Brac has a tiny population, and Little Cayman a mere handful of inhabitants. Grand Cayman is the largest island and the center of Caymanian life. The Caymans have many unusual characteristics—some of them unique—which make the islands fascinating, and make their waters a scuba diver's paradise.

The Caymanians have chosen to remain a British colony. Their government is a democracy of elected representatives, with the stabilizing influence of a governor and other appointed officials. By tradition, they pay none of the usual taxes such as income tax, sales tax, and real property tax. Government revenues are derived from business licenses, work permit fees, and customs duties (a hefty 20 percent on most items). Capitalism pervades the economic scene. There is ample opportunity for individual initiative, and many of the islanders are successful, self-made businessmen. International banking thrives on the Caymans' strict banking secrecy laws. Tourism is a vital, growing industry. Visitors come for the diving and other water sports, and for rest and relaxation on the beaches, especially the serenely beautiful "Seven Mile Beach."

A distinctive and delightful feature of the Caymans is the character of their people. Until the advent of regular air service in the early 'fifties, the islands were cut off from the rest of the world, and the Caymanians developed a culture all their own. During this time jobs were scarce, and the men went to sea, establishing a maritime tradition that is still strong. The islanders are descended from a variety of races and nationalities. They speak the English language in their own special way—a mixture of English, Welsh, and Caribbean English, spiced with colloquialisms. Warm friendliness and helpfulness are their trademark. Racism is almost non-existent. There is now growing concern that the unique character of the Caymanian culture may be lost in the islands' rapid transition from isolation to the mainstream of modern society.

The Cayman Islands are the flat tops of huge submerged mountains that loom up from the depths, just barely protruding above the surface. Below the surface, the sides of the mountains drop sheer for thousands of feet, and a few miles away the ocean floor plummets to 23,000 feet within the Cayman Trench—a vast chasm formed at the junction of the North American and Caribbean tectonic plates.

Many Caribbean islands are mountainous, with rushing streams and lush, tropical jungle. Water running off these islands carries silt into the ocean, where it is ingested by coral polyps that can neither digest nor excrete it, and are killed. The Caymans are basically flat, a large percentage of the land is mangrove swamp, and there are no streams at all. Most of the rainfall is absorbed by the soil and porous rock, or drains into the swamps. This topography above-water has made the islands unique underwater. With no silt to choke and kill their polyps, the coral reefs have grown uninhibited for thousands of years, producing unparalleled underwater scenery. The clarity of the silt-free water is extraordinary—underwater visibility is sometimes in excess of 200 feet.

While many animals thrive in the Caymanian waters, two groups—the gorgonians and the sponges—find the reefs a supremely suitable habitat, where they can flourish as nowhere else. The patch reefs and wall lips are gardens of gorgonians, abloom with sea fans, feather plumes, and sea whips—strange creatures that look like plants, but are colonies of tiny eight-tentacled animals. The size they attain here is testimony to the optimal growing conditions: many sea fans exceed 4 feet in diameter, while feather plumes and sea whips 6 feet tall are commonplace in some areas. The environment of the walls is exceptionally conducive to the growth of sponges. They throng the wall faces in an unsurpassable variety of types, colors, and forms—one of the ocean's greatest aggregations of these filter-feeding colonies.

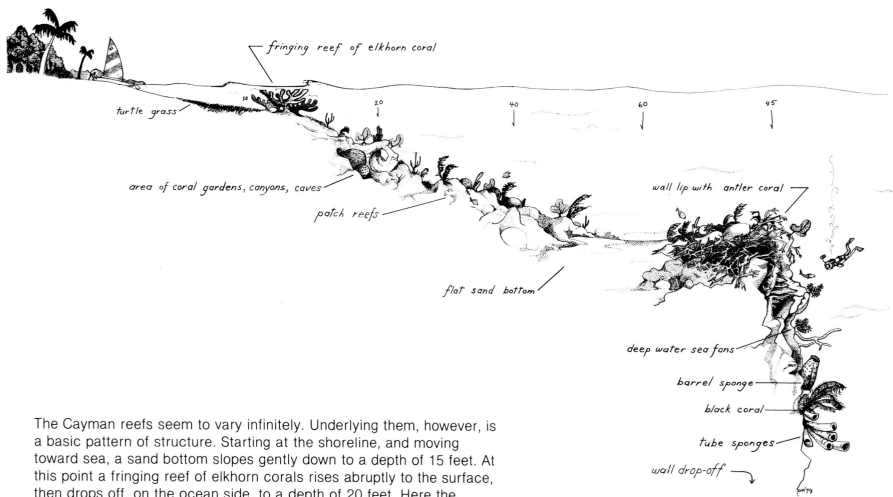

fringing reef of elkhorn coral

turtle grass

10　20　40　60　45

area of coral gardens, canyons, caves

patch reefs

flat sand bottom

wall lip with antler coral

deep water sea fans

barrel sponge

black coral

tube sponges

wall drop-off

Douglas Reed

The Cayman reefs seem to vary infinitely. Underlying them, however, is a basic pattern of structure. Starting at the shoreline, and moving toward sea, a sand bottom slopes gently down to a depth of 15 feet. At this point a fringing reef of elkhorn corals rises abruptly to the surface, then drops off, on the ocean side, to a depth of 20 feet. Here the bottom resumes its gradual downward trend. As it continues toward the sea, the slope is interrupted by numerous patch reefs, composed of hard-coral species. When the sand bottom reaches a depth of 50 to 65 feet, it comes to an end at the base of a steep hard-coral rise that forms the lip of the wall. The top of the lip may be as shallow as 30 feet, but is more often 40 or 50 feet below the surface.

The sea side of the lip is the brink of a cliff (commonly known as a wall) that plunges almost straight down for hundreds, even thousands, of feet. Each of the three islands is circumscribed by these great, underwater walls—immense, precipitous, and magnificent, they are one of the unique features of the islands' underwater world.

The wide diversity of diving locations around the Caymans can best be illustrated by describing several specific areas in detail.

George Town Harbor Reefs

George Town harbor is on the western side of the island, in the lee of prevailing winds. In its placid waters beautiful patch reefs have developed. Regretfully, their life and beauty have been reduced by heavy ship traffic, dumping of trash, construction of new port facilities, and the constant anchoring of ships. Even in a diminished state two of these reefs are well worth snorkeling and diving. They are most conveniently reached by dive-boat, but are within range of shore should a hearty snorkeler prefer to swim.

Soto's Reef is north of the harbor, about 200 yards offshore. The sand bottom at its base is 35 feet deep. From there the reef rises rapidly to a shallow 3 feet, its top crowned with delicate antler corals and jeweled with iridescent blue chromis and colorful wrasse. For the adventurous diver, many small caves honeycomb the reef, often filled with schools of shimmering silversides or copper-colored hatchetfish. Fish are plentiful. The small fish include most of the common reef species; the larger fish are usually members of the parrotfish family (page 5). Parrotfish are herbivores who feed on the algae that grow on coral. With their beak-like teeth they gnaw the coral to obtain the algae, and end up ingesting both. In their digestive tracts the coral is ground to fine sand, then excreted in arching streamers. Much of the Caribbean's lovely sand was milled in the guts of parrotfish.

South of the harbor, and only 100 yards offshore, is Eden Rock, a beautiful reef that rises from a 40-foot sand bottom to peaks within 6 feet of the surface. The top is closely packed with plate, lettuce, finger, and antler corals. Wherever there is a space between the corals, small flower-like zoanthids grow—delicate and intriguing little colonies that are all too often passed over unnoticed by divers. Within a colony, the tiny polyps are all similar in color; from colony to colony, their colors range widely, from Kelly green to iridescent orange. On top of Eden Rock, zoanthids of at least a dozen different colors can be seen. All around the reef are fierce little damselfish who guard their territories aggressively, chasing away intruders many times their size (page 6). They will even nip at divers who trespass within their boundaries. Poking a finger into a damselfish's territory will elicit a flurry of comic antics from the tiny firebrand, as it strives to eject the unwelcome invader. Eden Rock is riddled with winding tunnels and grottos, an intricate maze lit by shafts of sunlight that penetrate small rooftop openings, creating a blue, dream-like aura in the passages.

STOPLIGHT PARROTFISH
Feodor Pitcairn

DUSKY DAMSELFISH

BALBOA

Balboa Wreck

During a hurricane in 1932, the Norwegian freighter, Balboa, was thrown onto the rugged, stone iron-shore of George Town harbor. Pulled off the iron-shore, she sank in the harbor in 35 feet of water—a hazard to navigation. Eventually, she was blown up. Her twisted remains, scattered over the bottom, became a haven for all sorts of fish. Divers have an almost irresistible urge to dive on shipwrecks, and were naturally lured to the Balboa and her underwater residents (page 7). Soon the divers began attracting fish with bits of seafood and bread. Today, the pleasant pastime of fish-feeding has created a welfare state on the wreck, where an artificially large fish population subsists on handouts. The most voracious free-loaders are the yellow-and-black-striped sergeant majors, who swarm to greet each diver the moment he enters the water (page 9). Food triggers a frenzy. Once it has started, yellow-and-purple Spanish hogfish join in, along with a stray French angel or some yellowtail snappers.

Apart from the throngs in the feeding frenzy, many other fish can be seen around the Balboa. The peacock flounder changes color rapidly to match the bottom and often escapes a diver's notice, but there are always several about. Flounders are interesting, flattened fish that lie on one side and scoot along the bottom like hovercraft, stopping abruptly to twirl protruding, submarine periscope eyes. At night they may be found in full color, resting on the hull (p. 10). Many small groupers lurk in the background: the red hind, graysby (p. 11), and coney—each similarly spotted with red—all find the wreck's dense population a bountiful larder. Despite its brilliant coloring, the orange frogfish is well camouflaged and easy to miss (p. 12). Looking more like an orange sponge than a fish, this guy sits and waits for close-passing, unwary prey. Then suddenly: "Gulp."

The presence of a very large green moray eel gives divers an extra thrill (p. 13). Though ferocious in appearance and by reputation, this moray is really fairly tame. When offered pieces of raw fish, it has always been careful to take them very gingerly from the diver's hand. Once in a while, a majestic manta ray is sighted above the Balboa (p. 14). Called "Devil Fish" by old seamen because of its fearsome appearance, this giant creature poses no threat to man—it swims slowly through the water, feeding only on plankton.

For anyone diving in the Caymans, a dive on the Balboa is a must.

FEEDING FISH

GRAYSBY

PEACOCK FLOUNDER

Feodor Pitcairn

FROGFISH

GREEN MORAY

MANTA RAY

West Bay

From the north end of Seven Mile Beach, and west along the coast for about 2½ miles, is some of the finest drop-off diving on the island. From the lip down to 100 feet, the wall teems with life. Cutting through the lip are narrow, winding canyons with breathtaking archways, festooned with deepwater sea fans.

The drop-off has a high concentration of large barrel sponges that reproduce in a spectacular manner. The males resemble smoking volcanos, emitting bluish-white clouds of sperm; simultaneously, the females spew forth clusters of gametes like snowflakes, to be fertilized by chance encounter (pp. 16 & 17). Apparently this occurs only once a year, for about two hours, synchronized by some triggering mechanism still unknown. These giant sponges are so immense that underwater photographers often pose other divers in the picture for scale (p. 18).

Three locations are especially popular. The farthest west is "Orange Canyon," an area of many canyons and a rich, varied fauna, characterized by large orange plate sponges so large and prolific that at one point they coat an entire canyon wall with orange. One of "The Tunnel's" graceful archways is especially beautiful. It lies immersed in clear, deep-blue water at 100 feet. Its outer edges are encrusted with deepwater sea fans and colorful sponges, and deepwater sea fans have formed a lace-like covering over the crevice behind (p. 19). There, shy slender filefish hide and long-snouted trumpetfish hang nose down (p. 20). The most frequently dived location, "Trinity Caves," is well within the bay and very protected with a shallow 35-foot top and a fascinating series of winding crevices, 50 feet deep and so narrow that a diver need only extend his arms to touch both sides.

Behind the lip is a shallow white-sand area where sand dollars and sea biscuits lie just under the sand by day, and stingrays sometimes sleep on the bottom (p. 21). Patches of pencil-sized green garden eels, tails in their burrows, undulate gracefully together.

In the lee and close to many resorts, West Bay drop-off is heavily dived. The effects are already apparent. Coral is broken— unintentionally by clumsy divers, and intentionally by divers who think, "One little souvenir won't hurt." Several giant sponges and many large sea fans—organisms that take hundreds of years to grow—have been ripped out by anchors dropped indiscriminately by dive boats.

MALE BARREL SPONGE "SMOKING"

Paul Humann

FEMALE BARREL SPONGE

BARREL SPONGE AND DIVER

THE AUTHOR ABOVE THE SEA FANS

Feodor Pitcarin

TRUMPETFISH

STINGRAY

21

North Coast

The diving areas off Grand Cayman's north and south coasts are dived less frequently than those of the west coast because they are remote from the west side's many resorts and are subject to waves and weather conditions that sometimes make diving impossible.

From the north coast a large sound bites deeply into the island. North Sound is shallow; its bottom is covered mostly with turtle grass, and its circumference ringed by red mangrove swamp. Ecologically, it is extremely important—many of the island's oceanic animals begin their lives in the sound. The protected waters are a natural breeding ground for fish and other marine life. The tangled mangrove roots are a haven where juvenile fish and other tiny creatures grow, protected from their predators, until they are ready to move to the nearby reefs.

A fringing reef extends across the sound's entire sea exposure. On its protected side are sand flats. The flats appear desolate, but have many intriguing tenants. Caribbean conch, helmet shells, sunbursts, the occasional trumpet triton, and many other molluscs dwell on this bottom. Empty conch shells are homes for hermit crabs. Sand tilefish build tunnel-homes from broken pieces of coral and fragments of shell. Tiny sailfin blennies live in small holes, with only their heads sticking out to watch for food. When a tempting particle floats by, the blenny jumps out of its hole, oversized dorsal fin flicking in quick little bursts and delicate pelvic fins working in rhythm (p. 23). It nabs the food and returns with equal speed. The entire excursion takes only a couple of seconds. To photograph a sailfin blenny is no simple chore. The photographer first has to find a blenny hiding in its hole, and then must wait quietly until it no longer feels threatened (a good 20 minutes). Finally, he must snap the picture during the blenny's sudden, two-second appearance. Success is more a matter of luck than skill.

The six-mile fringing reef, rising to the surface from a sand bottom of only 15 feet, provides excellent, extremely shallow diving. Stout arms of elkhorn coral shape the reef's bulwark (p. 24). They are closely woven, forming innumerable small holes, grottos, and passageways—ideal sanctuaries for little fish. As a result, the reef teems with schools of small fish of every type, particularly grunts and margates. Nocturnal squirrelfish, seeking dark crannies by day, inhabit the coral crevices (p. 25). Deeper, darker holes harbor Caribbean lobster.

SAILFIN BLENNY

23

FRINGING REEF WITH DIVER

Paul Humann

SQUIRRELFISH

Feodor Pitcairn

24

The north coast is famed for the ''Great Wall of Cayman;'' which parallels its shore. Many divers do not realize that the Great Wall extends not only outside the North Sound fringing reef, but along the entire north coast. The brink of the wall is 40 to 60 feet deep. From there, great cliffs drop into the ocean's abyss, broken with beautiful canyons, tunnels, fissures, and archways.

The cliff tops are capped with delicate antler coral and a bewildering array of gorgonians that grow to an extraordinary size. One giant amongst the towering feather plumes is over 10 feet tall (p. 27). Gorgonians, unlike corals, have eight-tentacled polyps that are open night and day, each individual as graceful and lovely as the colony to which it belongs (p. 28). Flamingo tongue shells browse on the gorgonians, extremely handsome with their leopard-spotted mantles extended over their shells (p. 29). When they sense danger these gastropods retract their mantles, exposing disappointingly dowdy shells, cream-colored and plain. Fish are everywhere, all sizes. The hamlets are particularly abundant. This wall top is one of the few places where the rare shy hamlet can be found (p. 30).

But do not stop on the brink—the best is yet to come. Plummeting almost straight down, bathed in hues of blue, the cliff walls reach deeper and deeper shades, until lost from view in darkness.

At first, the diver is overwhelmed by the grandeur. Only later can he focus on the luxuriant growth on the wall. The outer edges are covered with deepwater sea fans. From as shallow as 60 feet, down to 150, graceful black coral trees embellish the wall (p. 31). Slow-growing, this bushy ''sea tree'' is in danger of extinction on the island. It is highly prized by the jewelry industry, and by divers who think their machismo is enhanced by a black coral trophy. The mystique of black coral is based on fairy tales: ''It's found only at tremendous depths.''— absolutely untrue, in Cayman it grows at normal everyday diving depths; ''It's rare!''—also untrue, until recently it was fairly common around most Caribbean islands. Sadly, black coral is becoming rare, simply because those taking it are not allowing time for its slow growth rate to keep pace. Neither government nor jewelers seem to appreciate that black coral is a valuable natural resource, that it could last forever if properly harvested and conserved, but that, at the present rate of taking, it could be destroyed in less than ten years.

DIVER WITH FEATHER PLUME

Paul Humann

GORGONIAN POLYPS

FLAMINGO TONGUE

Paul Humann

DIVER WITH BLACK CORAL

SHY HAMLET

Feodor Pitcairn

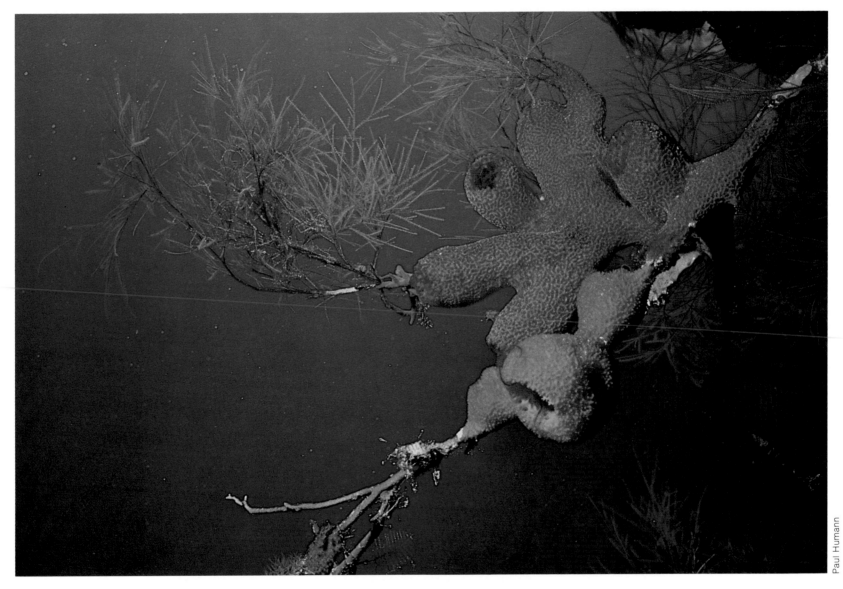

RED CUP SPONGES ON BLACK CORAL

Paul Humann

HYDROID COLONY ON RED SPONGE

BROWN TUBE SPONGE

ORANGE TUBE SPONGE

Feodor Pitcairn

34

Clinging to the limbs of the black coral trees are brilliant red cup sponges—the most resplendent, prolific array of this species in the Caribbean (p. 32). In natural light they appear deep burgundy, as the water filters out the red end of the spectrum from the sunlight. Turn on a diver's light, and the effect is electrifying. As if by magic, muted burgundy is transformed to the most dazzling reds imaginable. Another striking type of sponge, the rope sponge, hangs from the wall like tangled rope, brown, red, or purple. Hydroid colonies often attach themselves to rope sponges (p. 33). They form intriguing, delicate designs, so tiny they are easily overlooked. The environmental conditions on the wall are ideal for sponges. They grow on the wall-face in untold numbers, and in a fascinating variety of species. Exploring the wall, more and more kinds can be seen: fat brown tube sponges (p. 34), tall orange tube sponges (p. 35), and frilly azure vase sponges, in lavender and pink (p. 37).

Beneath the wall's overhanging ledges dwell a wide variety of life-forms. "Daddy-long-legs"—cute little long-nosed arrow crabs—clamber over corals on spidery, gangling appendages (p. 38). Hanging from the ceilings are fiery-red gorgonians tufted with snow-white polyps (p. 39). Seafrost colonies dangle from the rocks like tiny, white Christmas decorations (p. 40). Intricate bryozoan colonies swirl against the ceiling, reminiscent of a silversmith's designs (p. 41). Ornately patterned encrusting sponges make a backdrop for them all (p. 42).

Once I sighted a pair of spotted eagle rays, winging lazily along the wall like sentinels (p. 43). In unison they gracefully soared, arced, turned, swept downward, and then powerfully stroked back up. Even during the day, when they are resting, these large creatures must keep cruising, forced to swim constantly in order to keep water passing through their gills; at night, they patrol the shallow sand bottoms, hunting for the molluscs upon which they feed.

AZURE VASE SPONGE

ARROW CRAB AT NIGHT

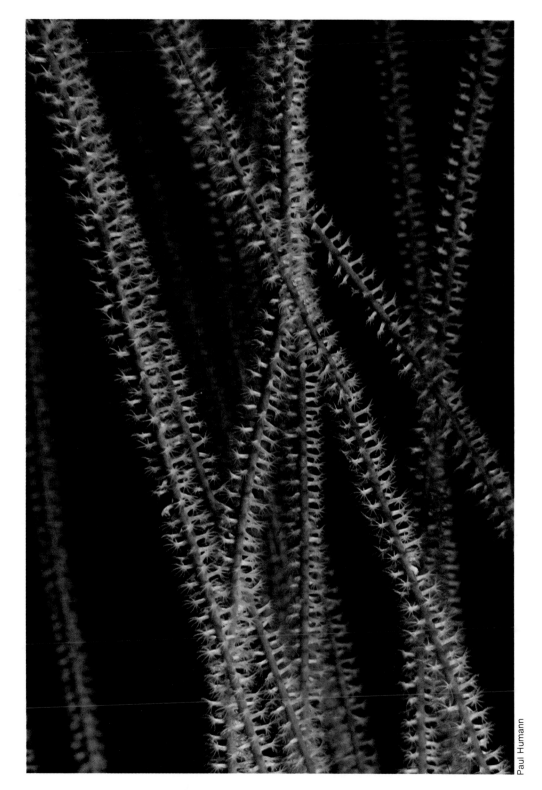

RED "PIPE CLEANER" GORGONIANS

Paul Humann

39

SEA FROST

BRYOZOAN COLONIES

ENCRUSTING SPONGES

Paul Humann

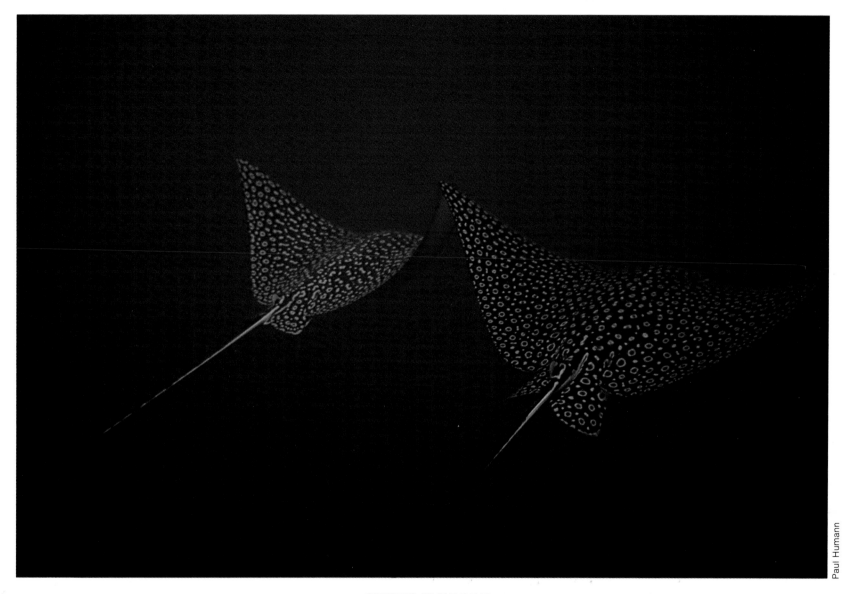

SPOTTED EAGLE RAYS

South Coast

The south coast of Grand Cayman resembles the north in several respects: its entire coastline is also paralleled by a jagged sheer wall; its marine fauna is similar. But some aspects differ. The south coast does not have a large sound like North Sound, but has several smaller sounds and bays. Washed year-round by a prevailing swell from the southeast, the fringing reefs off these sounds are even more spectacular than the north's, as the surge enhances the growth of impressive stands of elkhorn corals (p. 45). The sweep of the swell across the reefs sets large sea fans swaying, their lacy, yellow or purple faces turned into the surge to capture the food it carries (p. 46).

Great fingers of coral reach from the fringing reef out toward the ocean, forming between them narrow canyons and winding pathways of sand. Once, as I was entering a sand area between the fingers, my eye was caught by the glint of hundreds of silvery fish. They turned, and encircled me in a whirling doughnut—now ghostly, now gleaming as the sunlight caught their sides. They looked like barracuda, which made me slightly nervous. But I kept my camera clicking (p. 47). They were, in fact, the barracuda's cousins—schooling southern sennets. Caves and tunnels twist through the fingers. At Spots Bay, and the west end of Bodden Bay, there are several large tunnels and caves, which are sometimes filled with vast, mesmerizing schools of dwarf herrings. As a diver (or large fish) passes through, the school opens, contours, closes, and flows about him (p. 48).

There are many patch reefs between the fringing reefs and the wall. One, off Southwest Point, is site of the famous "Tarpon Alley." From 20 to 40 feet down, it forms twisting canyons, overhangs, caves, and arches. The rugged seascape is constantly raked by ocean currents which come around the point, sweeping in nutrients necessary to the food chain and washing away debris; marine life, therefore, abounds. In the canyons, large schools of night-feeding tarpon rest by day, protected from the current (p. 49). They are majestic creatures, up to 8 feet long, gleaming as if sculpted of stainless steel.

SUNBURST

SEA FAN

SOUTHERN SENNETS

Paul Humann

47

SILVER CLOUD

TARPON

One beautifully calm Monday morning, I was diving near Southwest Point. I was on the bottom, photographing a cooperative spadefish, when—quite subliminally—I became aware of something watching me. Suddenly, something large moved within my peripheral vision. I spun about. A huge jewfish was swimming slowly toward me—a monster easily 6 feet long, that must have weighed over 400 pounds. It ambled by, obviously curious, then allowed me and my companions to follow, for twenty minutes or more. At times it even permitted us to come alongside and touch. I was so excited, I nearly forgot to take pictures. When I remembered, I had to keep backing away to get the whole fish in the photograph (p. 51). Eventually we ran low on air, and had to leave. We surfaced exhausted.

On the south coast, the sand bottom behind the wall lip is much deeper than on the north; the lip is, therefore, much taller, and the crevices and canyons cutting through it, more dramatic. Around Spots, Breakers, and just west of Old Isaacs, coral has overgrown the canyons to form winding tunnels. Enter one of these tunnels from the shore side of the lip—it winds down in darkness, with only occasional shafts of light slanting through small breaks in the ceiling. As it nears the wall opening, the tunnel begins to glow with an aura of electric blue. Suddenly the tunnel ends in the open water at 100 feet or more— below, the wall is plunging straight down to the nothingness of the abyss; above, it rises toward the sun. Divers soar across the face of an apparently bottomless cliff, more like birds than humans.

Along the wall face are multitudes of deepwater sea fans. Here and there black coral trees grow. Clinging to the undersides of ledges are pink-and-lavender hydroid colonies (commonly known as Ming coral) and occasional spiny oysters, encrusted with red and orange sponge. Clam-like file shells are tucked in little fissures. When open, they display scarlet lips and streaming white tentacles, bringing fireworks to mind (p. 52). In among the crowding animals may be a little plant, the sea pearl—its tiny lustrous sphere, one of the biggest cells known. Divers' bubbles attract schools of horse-eye jacks, who come in for a closer look (p. 53). The silvery glint of bubbles also attracts the fearsome-looking, ever-present barracuda (p. 54). While the barracuda will not harm a scuba diver, it has the disconcerting habit of barreling straight at him as if to attack, stopping short a few feet away to bare its teeth menacingly and work its jaws. Then, unnervingly, it will stalk the diver until at last it gets bored with its game.

GIANT JEWFISH

Paul Humann

FIREWORKS

52

HORSE-EYE JACKS

BARRACUDA

East End

The land rises on East End afford a dramatic view of the fringing reef that encloses the eastern end of Grand Cayman. Look to sea, over the calm, turquoise-blue waters of Gun Bay. Churning white lines of waves break on the reef, punctuated by two large, rusting shipwrecks that sit high above water; far beyond, deep ocean blue meets the blue of the sky. This scene is the setting for extensive coral gardens, a delightful place to spend an afternoon of diving. There is a wealth of things to see and time to enjoy them at leisure, for air supplies last longer at shallow depths, permitting the luxury of extra diving time.

A short distance out from the fringing reef, narrow canyons twist and intertwine to form a labyrinth. Within the canyons dwell schools of the small reclusive fish that seek out dimly lit places. Juveniles of many species take refuge from their predators in these natural sanctuaries. Lobsters and large reef crabs hide in the dark recesses.

On the shallow reef tops, thousands of small fish flicker in and out among the sea fans and majestic elkhorn corals. Blue chromis swarm everywhere, like fields of blue flowers, each lustrous little fish gleaming against the background (p. 56). Several species of angelfish and butterflyfish forage gracefully about the reefs, often traveling in pairs. The butterflyfish's markings are protective: large false "eyes" on a foureye butterfly's tail apparently divert attack from its head; dark bars disrupt the outline of the banded butterfly (pp. 57 & 58). The friendliest fish on the reef are the angelfish. They are curious and often approach human beings—grey angels have been known to come and nibble at divers' bubbles. French angelfish are dramatically colored, with delicate gold rims highlighting their very dark scales (p. 59). The grey angels' coloring is subtle, shades of tan and grey (p. 60); while the queen angelfish are resplendent in luminous blue and gold, with a brilliant circlet of blue on their brows (Frontispiece). Lurking in the shadows are Nassau groupers, shifting color to blend with the background (p. 61). Groupers gather here in such great numbers that one part of the reef is called "Grouper Grotto."

The east end is the windward side of the island, and is subject to heavy waves and surge action that sometimes make diving unpleasant, if not impossible. Unlucky divers must try to take solace in the fact that this turbulence, though it spoils their plans, is the very factor that makes the east end such a beautiful place to dive.

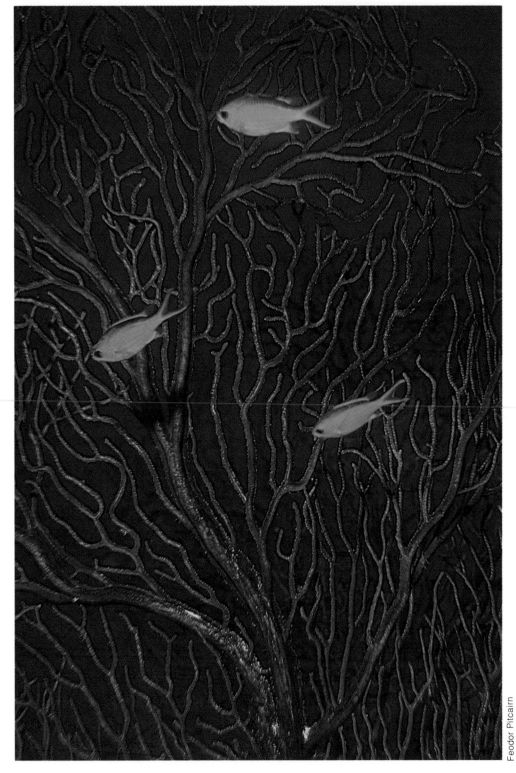

BLUE CHROMIS AND SEA FAN

FOUREYE BUTTERFLYFISH

FRENCH ANGELFISH

Overleaf ►
GRAY ANGELFISH
Feodor Pitcairn

Ten Mile Banks

Just west of Grand Cayman Island the bottom drops to a depth of 3,600 feet, but ten miles out it comes up abruptly, within 80 feet of the surface, forming a bank approximately five miles long and half a mile wide. "Ten Mile Banks" is a favorite fishing ground for Caymanian fishermen. Their stories about vast numbers of large fish inspired a try at diving the banks, despite all warnings of strong currents and shark activity. The warnings about currents were valid. But during several dozen dives only one shark appeared—a nurse shark.

To dive the "Ten Mile Banks" is novel and exciting. The water out there is always clear—it is, for all practical purposes, open ocean. Entering the water, the diver sinks downward, his senses coming alive as he finds himself completely enveloped in clear, cobalt blue. (In normal reef diving, such intensely blue water is seen only off to one side, if at all.) Far below are the banks—the diver floats down, like a sky-diver floating toward earth.

The bottom is flat, and is raked by strong currents, against which divers must constantly work to avoid being swept beyond reach of the boat. Breaking the bottom's monotony is one of the greatest aggregations of giant barrel sponges anywhere. Many of them are several feet wide and more than 6 feet high. Scurrying about are many of the more common small reef fish, and several species that are uncommon elsewhere around the islands, such as the beautiful violet-and-yellow cherubfish, and the sargassum triggerfish with intricate tracings of iridescent blue (p. 63).

Occasional coral mounds rise as high as 20 feet above the bottom. About them gather snappers, and Nassau groupers up to 40 pounds. Large numbers of yellowfin jacks flow around and above the mounds; swirling schools of horse-eye jacks sweep by. It is easy to see what brings the fishermen to these banks. A diver can just sit back, part of the cobalt blue backdrop, and watch all the activity. Time passes quickly on this deep plateau. Too soon, his pressure gauge and decompression meter are warning the diver that he must leave.

◀ Overleaf

NASSAU GROUPER

Feodor Pitcairn

SARGASSUM TRIGGERFISH

Paul Humann

63

Cayman Brac

Seventy miles east-northeast of Grand Cayman is Cayman Brac, the most scenic of the Cayman Islands. Only two miles wide, the island is twelve miles long, running from northeast to southwest. Its topography is unusual for a Caymanian island for while the southwest end is flat, the land rises with increasing abruptness toward the northeast end, where sheer limestone cliffs, 140 feet high, plunge dramatically into the sea. Waves, pounding constantly against the cliffs, thwart significant coral development. The long northern and southern coasts, however, have drop-offs similar to those off Grand Cayman.

Although the wall off Cayman Brac's north coast is not as sheer as Grand Cayman's, it has an impressive beauty of its own. Through the drop-off lip, large sand canyons cut their way like white rivers. Large patch reefs abound. The south coast has many coral gardens. Huge stands of elkhorn coral form narrow canyons, tunnels, and caves.

Under little pressure from divers and fishermen, the waters of Cayman Brac teem with marine life. The bright-spotted flatworms seldom leave their homes within the coral tangles, so it is exciting to see one making an excursion in the open (p. 65). Tightly knit schools of blue tang flow about the corals, pausing to graze on lush growths of algae (p. 66). The blue tang looks vulnerable, but has an unusual means of defense: a razor-sharp spine at the base of its tail that can be quickly erected to slash an aggressor. The slow-moving smooth trunkfish, potentially easy prey, has also evolved an off-beat device for protection (p. 67). It builds a carapace of bony plates around its body and swims about the reef in a box—funny looking, but effective.

When exploring, inspect the tube sponges carefully—they are the homes of all sorts of creatures. Small shrimp are common inhabitants. They hide inside, poking just their antennae out the opening (p. 68). Gobies sit in the mouths of the tubes as though sunning themselves on their doorsteps; if danger appears, they retreat into the sponges' recesses (p. 69). Sea anemones are also used as dwellings—little crabs, fish, or shrimp live within the protection of their stinging tentacles. Tenants of the pink-tipped anemones are amply quartered, for their hosts are often a foot across, and well supplied with long, brightly-tipped tentacles (p. 70).

The reefs of Cayman Brac have never been heavily dived. Their natural, virgin beauty is delightful to experience.

FLATWORM

Overleaf ►
BLUE TANG
Feodor Pitcairn

65

Paul Humann

SHRIMP IN TUBE SPONGE

◄ Overleaf

SMOOTH TRUNKFISH

Feodor Pitcairn

GOBY IN TUBE SPONGE

PINK-TIPPED SEA ANEMONE

Feodor Pitcairn

FINGER CORAL POLYPS AND FEATHER WORM

Little Cayman

Only seven miles from Cayman Brac is the island of Little Cayman. The best and the worst diving areas in the Caymans can be found off its shores: most are, at best, mediocre; two are magnificent.

The first is on the east end. The reef structure is unusual: the top of the drop-off is shallow and very close to the fringing reef, creating a fantastic ledge between the rising fringing reef and the wall's brink. Covering the ledge are enormous stands of flower coral, interspersed with patches of fragile lettuce and finger coral. Between the coral fingers it is sometimes possible to glimpse the dainty crescent of a serpulid feather worm's tentacles, before it whisks them back into its tube (p. 71). The ledge has the best of everything in one small package—fringing reef, coral garden, and sheer wall, all on one dive.

The second area is even more exciting. In fact, it has to be one of the best diving areas in the world. From Jackson Point through Bloody Bay (the site of a fierce pirate battle), and southwest for another two miles, lies a diver's paradise. The drop-off is embellished with canyons, caves, tunnels, and crevices—a rugged terrain ornamented with deepwater sea fans, black coral trees, giant barrel sponges, and the longest, purplest tube sponges ever. Divers can wind their way through tunnel after tunnel, down from the sand flats, and out through the wall face, suspended above the abyss (p. 73).

The reef tops are shallow and covered with sea fans and sea plumes. Tangled thickets of antler coral are havens for schools of juvenile fish. Notches in coral outcroppings provide refuge for larger fish. In one niche I found an unhappy parrotfish sequestered, reluctant host to a sharksucker that lacked a bigger, more suitable fish (p. 74). One sharksucker seeking a host adopted my boat. Each diver that entered the water received the fish's unwelcome attentions. Each time it was firmly rejected and returned to the hull.

On the sand flats behind the lip live many shellfish, including (for the initiate) delicious Caribbean conch. Stingrays dig in the sand for food, their wings throwing up great clouds, which fall on their backs, making them almost invisible. Bar jacks hover above, waiting for any stray morsels. Jellyfish float near the surface, rhythmically pumping their bells. On first seeing one species, I thought, "Weird! That crazy mixed-up jellyfish is swimming upside down!" But this jellyfish very sanely turns over to expose the algae in its tentacles to the sunlight, so they can grow (p. 75). Apparently the algae are the jellyfish's food.

LITTLE CAYMAN WALL

PARROTFISH AND SHARKSUCKER

UPSIDE-DOWN JELLYFISH

The section of wall southwest of Bloody Bay is one of the "Seven Wonders" of the underwater world. From an extreme shallow of 20 feet, the bottom suddenly plunges 1,000 feet straight down. The face of the precipice, as sheer as a skyscraper, drops into the blue, luring a diver downward. He glides past huge black coral trees, decorated with vivid red and orange cup sponges and ornamental balls of sea frost. Tall stovepipe sponges, intensely yellow, glow against the deep blue of the ocean (p. 77); great tube sponges jut out like an array of trumpets (p. 78); red and purple rope sponges hang in serpentine contortions. Familiar fish look strange, oriented to the vertical wall face as though it were a horizontal bottom. The entire wall is covered with living things: colorful encrusting sponges, large flower corals, swirling bryozoans, and ribbons of green and purple algae—bizarre splashes of color like paints on an artist's pallet.

The awesome visual experience (piqued by a touch of nitrogen narcosis from diving so deep) gives the diver one of life's all-time highs. But soon his mind must snap back to reality. He has been down too deep, too long, and must return to the shallows for decompression to avoid the bends. At such great depths a diver's blood absorbs abnormal amounts of nitrogen; by stopping at shallow depths he can vent the nitrogen naturally. Usually decompression means hanging on the anchor rope with nothing to do—a very boring process. Above the wall of Little Cayman, the wall-top is so shallow that divers spend their decompression time happily exploring—and what a spot to explore.

Organisms crowd the flat wall-top, competing so fiercely for growing space that one often overgrows the other. Purple fans, sea whips, and feather plumes sway with the surge, as a forest stirs in the breeze. Colonies of white-and-lavender feather-dusters arrange themselves artistically in flowery bouquets (p. 79). Each pretty circlet is the tentacles of a single tube-dwelling worm, protruded to gather food and the debris that the worm uses to build its parchment tube. Closely related, a serpulid tube worm—the Christmas-tree worm—burrows into coral heads, and extends into the open twin spiral plumes (p. 80). Should their light-and-pressure-sensitive cells detect danger, the worm retracts them precipitously. Octopus may slink about, even in broad daylight. Great schools of blue and midnight parrotfish munch on algae-covered coral. Little fish swarm.

STOVEPIPE SPONGE

TRUMPET SPONGE

FEATHER-DUSTERS

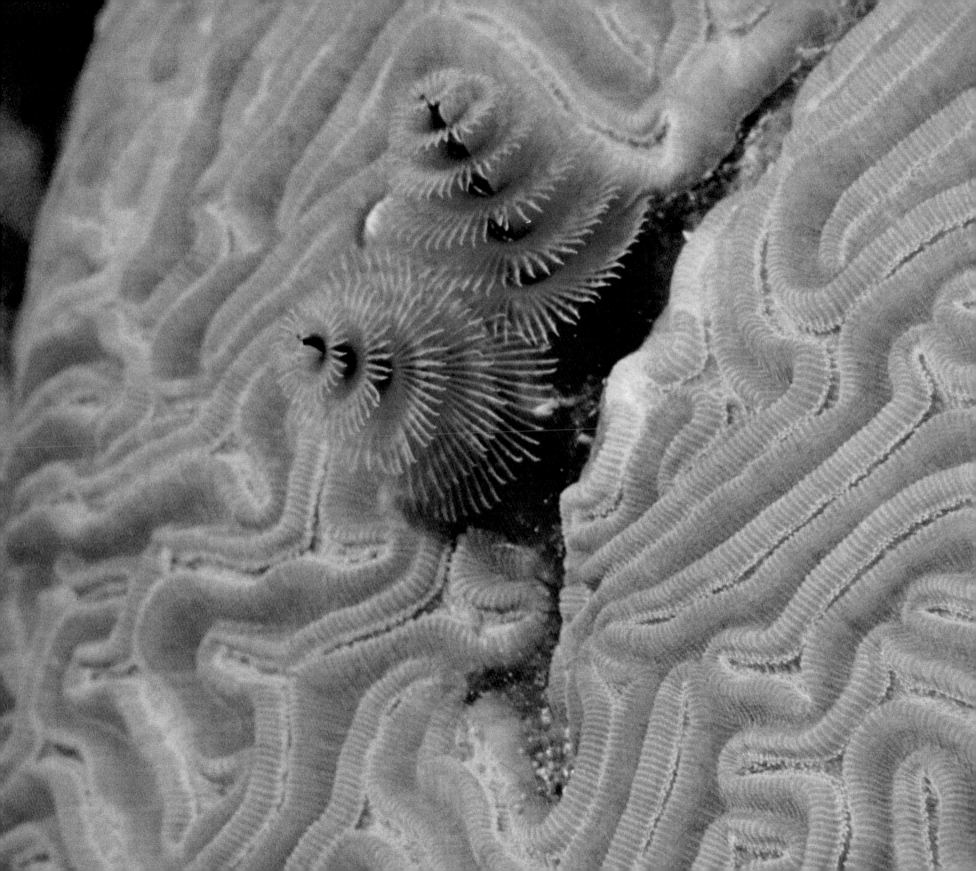

There are established cleaning stations around the reef where shrimp, gobies, and other little fish offer their services to clean larger fish by picking off small parasites, damaged tissue, and debris (pp. 82 & 83). At rest, little blennies prop themselves up on their delicate pelvic fins— a characteristic stance that gives them stability even in the face of strong currents. The diamond blenny is impervious to the sea anemones' stinging nematocysts, which paralyze most small fish that touch them; it can, therefore, perch with impunity right in the midst of the deadly tentacles, where no predator dares attack it (p. 84).

There always seems to be a red hind somewhere about, discretely stationed to watch a diver's every move (p. 85). The red hind, like most groupers, is a hermaphrodite that first matures as a female and later switches, to function as a male for the rest of its life.

Diving at night is always a treat. A night dive on Little Cayman's wall top is especially exciting. The underwater world does not quiet down at nightfall. While most daytime creatures are hidden, sleeping, those of the night come out, and busily hunt for food, so divers can see many an animal they could never see by day. Basket starfish climb high on the corals, in search of advantageous positions for feeding. Gorgonians spread their tangled arms to snare floating plankton. The night-feeding hard-coral polyps are now open in their millions, bringing the beauty of fairyland to the nighttime reef. The flower coral's exquisite polyps display translucent, star-tipped tentacles (p. 86). Black, long-spined sea urchins forage over the reef in unexpected numbers, and lobsters and large reef crabs are out for a nighttime stroll.

Many fish are mesmerized by a light beam. In a trance, they submit to being touched; some appear to enjoy being stroked. As dive-lights pass over the reef, stabs of color leap out. The red sponges are dramatic— unobtrusive and unnoticed in daylight, they suddenly appear to be everywhere under the lights at night. Attaching themselves to red sponges, white hydroid colonies create underwater Christmas decorations all the year round (p. 87). Occasionally, a sweeping light will glint off something out in the open water—a clue to the possible presence of squid (p. 88). It is worth swimming over to see, for the highly intelligent squid are graceful and unusual. A night dive reveals a fascinating, altogether different aspect of the underwater world; it is an adventure which every experienced diver should try.

◄ CHRISTMAS-TREE WORM
Feodor Pitcairn

GRAYSBY WITH CLEANING SHRIMP

SQUIRRELFISH WITH CLEANING GOBY

Overleaf ▶
DIAMOND BLENNY IN SEA ANEMONE

Feodor Pitcairn

Paul Humann

FLOWER CORAL AT NIGHT

◄ Overleaf
RED HIND
Feodor Pitcairn

CHRISTMAS HYDROID

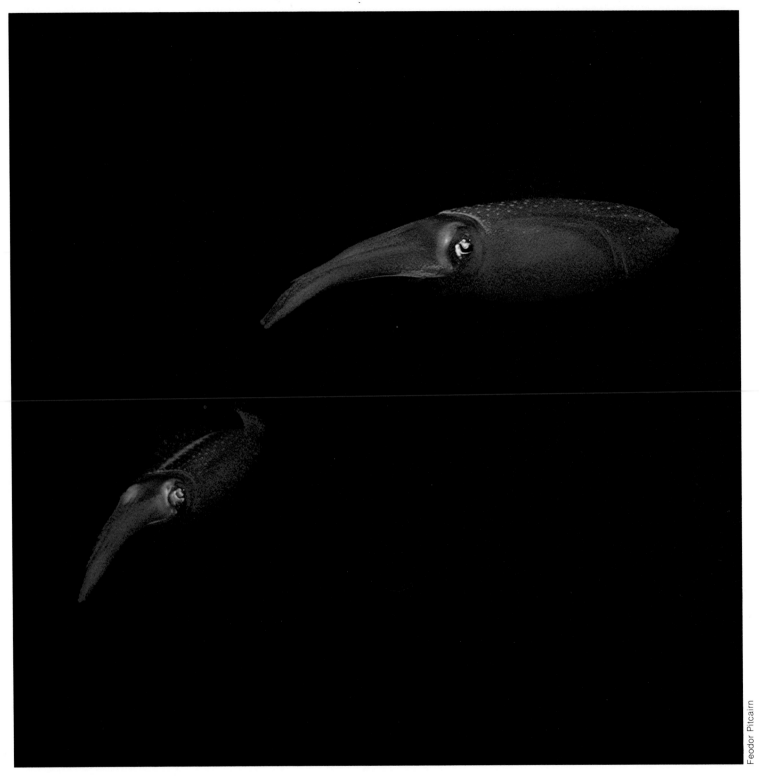

SQUID

Epilogue

The excitement of a living reef is the exhilaration which comes when one experiences true wilderness, or the "sense of wonder" which comes when one gazes at our galaxy on a clear night.

We "civilized" men badly need this tonic to compensate for the sterility of our synthetic environment. All too often, man has so obliterated the natural systems which prevailed before his coming, that he has lost any keen perception of their remarkable order and function.

The community of animals constituting a living reef abounds in what appears to be an infinite array of forms, colors, and functions. At first, one is captivated by the flitting scenery of colorful fish. Later one comes to appreciate the intricate chains of interdependence which exist between the very smallest and the largest life-forms on the reef.

One finds curious symbiotic relationships, such as the diamond blenny who makes his home among the stinging tentacles of a sea anemone, or the "cleaning station," where a predatory grouper establishes such a remarkable rapport with the small fish cleaning him of parasites that they can enter his mouth without fear.

The hunter may become the hunted. Bizarre forms of mimicry take place. Everywhere the reef is ruled by strict observance of territory. Courtships assume a variety of patterns, even within one species, as with the stoplight parrotfish.

Only in recent years has modern diving equipment made it possible to enjoy this relatively unexplored environment. Yet the coral reefs, like the world's rain forests, are already seriously threatened by mankind. The threat takes many forms, from the thoughtless collecting of sea creatures, to sewage outfalls which destroy entire reefs by discharging large quantities of nutrients, thereby triggering rampant algae growth. Population pressures cause other problems. When silt from construction sites is washed into the ocean, it has a devastating effect on marine life. The myriads of chemicals released into the sea can also kill the delicate organisms of the reefs.

One must hold to the hope that what man comes to love and hold dear, he will endeavor to protect. With love comes understanding, which must be translated into sound management policies.

Feodor U. Pitcairn

Page No.	Common Name	Scientific Name (*In Italics*)
frontis-piece	Queen Angelfish	*Holacanthus ciliaris*
5.	Stoplight Parrotfish	*Sparisoma viride*
	Sea Fan	*Iciligorgia schrammi* Duchassaing
6.	Dusky Damselfish	*Eupomacentrus dorsopunicans*
	Orange Tube Sponge	*Verongia (= Aplysina) fistularis* (Pallas)
9.	Sergeant Major	*Abudefduf saxatilis*
	Spanish Hogfish	*Bodianus rufus*
10.	Peacock Flounder	*Bothus lunatus*
11.	Graysby	*Petrometopon cruentatum*
12.	Island Frogfish	*Antennarius bermudensis*
	Sponge	*Verongula (Verongia) gigantea* (Hyatt)
13.	Green Moray	*Gymnothorax funebris*
14.	Manta Ray	*Manta birostris*
16.	Barrel Sponge	*Xestospongia muta* (Schmidt)
17.	Barrel Sponge	*Xestospongia muta* (Schmidt)
18.	Barrel Sponge	*Xestospongia muta* (Schmidt)
20.	Trumpetfish	*Aulostomus maculatus*
21.	Southern Stingray	*Dasyatis americana*
23.	Sailfin Blenny	*Emblemaria pandionis*
24.	Predominant: Elkhorn Coral	*Acropora palmata* (Lamarck)
	Also: Brain Coral	*Diploria* sp.
25.	Squirrelfish	*Holocentrus rufus*
27.	Feather Plume Gorgonian	*Pseudopterogorgia acerosa*
28.	Gorgonian Polyps	*Briareum asbestinum* (Pallas)
29.	Flamingo Tongue	*Cyphoma gibbosum* Linnaeus
30.	Shy Hamlet	*Hypoplectrus guttavarius*
	Staghorn Coral	*Acropora cervicornis* (Lamarck)
31.	Black Coral	Order: *Antipatharia*
32.	Red Cup Sponges	*Mycale* sp. (not yet described)
33.	Hydroid	Order: *Hydroidea*
	Sponge	*Haliclona rubens* (Pallas)
34.	Brown Tube Sponge	*Agelas schmidtii* Wilson
	Juvenile Bluehead	*Thalassoma bifasciatum*
	Upper right: Fire Coral	*Millepora alcicornis*
35.	Orange Tube Sponge	*Verongia (= Aplysina) fistularis* (Pallas)
	Left: Brain Coral	*Diploria labyrinthiformis* (Linnaeus)
	Lower center: Yellow-gold Encrusting Sponge bordering Star Coral	*Mycale laevis* (Carter)
37.	Azure Vase Sponge	*Callyspongia plicifera* (Lamarck)
	Staghorn Coral	*Acropora cervicornis*
38.	Arrow Crab	*Stenorhynchus seticornis*
	Left: Sea Fan	*Iciligorgia schrammi* Duchassaing
	Right: Red Rope Sponge	*Haliclona rubens* (Pallas)
	Orange Sponge	*Mycale laevis* (Carter)
39.	"Pipe Cleaner" Gorgonians	*Nicella schmitti*
40.	Sea Frost	Unidentifiable
41.	Bryozoan Colonies	Phylum: *Bryozoa*; Class: *ectoprocta*
	Orange Encrusting Sponges	? *Spirastrella coccinea* (Duchassaing & Michelotti)

Page No.	Common Name	Scientific Name (*In Italics*)
42.	Encrusting Sponge	? *Halisarca* sp.
43.	Spotted Eagle Rays	*Aetobatus narinari*
45.	Elkhorn Coral	*Acropora palmata* (Lamarck)
46.	Sea Fan	*Gorgonia flabellum*
47.	Southern Sennets	*Sphyraena picudilla*
48.	Dwarf Herring	*Jenkinsia lamprotaenia*
49.	Tarpon	*Megalops atlanticus*
51.	Giant Jewfish	*Epinephelus itajara*
52.	"Fireworks"	*Lima scabra*
53.	Horse-eye Jacks	*Caranx latus*
54.	Great Barracuda	*Sphyraena barracuda*
56.	Blue Chromis	*Chromis cyaneus*
	Sea Fan	*Iciligorgia schrammi* Duchassaing
57.	Foureye Butterflyfish	*Chaetodon capistratus*
	Left: Corky Sea Fingers	*Briareum asbestinum* (Pallas)
	Right: Fire Coral	*Millepora alcicornis*
58.	Banded Butterflyfish	*Chaetodon striatus*
59.	French Angelfish	*Pomacanthus paru*
60.	Gray Angelfish	*Pomacanthus arcuatus*
61.	Nassau Grouper	*Epinephelus striatus*
	Sponge	*Neofibularia nolitangere* (Duchassaing & Michelotti)
63.	Sargassum Triggerfish	*Xanthichthys ringens*
65.	Flatworm	*Pseudoceros pardalis*
	Sponge	*Mycale* sp. (not yet described)
66.	Blue Tang	*Acanthurus coeruleus*
67.	Smooth Trunkfish	*Lactophrys triqueter*
68.	Shrimp	*Hippolysmata wurdemanni*
	Sponge	*Callyspongia (Spinosella) vaginalis* (Lamarck)
69.	Goby	*Gobiosoma horsti*
	Sponge	*Callyspongia (Spinosella) vaginalis* (Lamarck)
70.	Sea Anemone	*Condylactis gigantea* (Weinland)
71.	Feather Worm	*Pomatostegus stellatus* (Abildgaard)
	Finger Coral	*Porites porites* (Pallas)
74.	Rainbow Parrotfish	*Scarus guacamaia*
	Sharksucker	*Echeneis naucrates*
75.	Upside-down Jellyfish	*Cassiopeia xamachana*
77.	Stovepipe Sponge	*Verongia aurea*
	Bicolor Damselfish	*Eupomacentrus partitus*
78.	Trumpet Sponge	*Verongia (Aplysina) archeri* (Higgin)
79.	Feather-Duster Worms	Phylum: *Annelida*; Order: *sabellida*
80.	Christmas-Tree Worm	*Spirobranchus giganteus*
	Brain Coral	*Diploria labyrinthiformis* (Linnaeus)
82.	Graysby	*Petrometopon cruentatum*
	Cleaner Shrimp	*Periclimenes pedersoni*
83.	Longjaw Squirrelfish	*Holocentrus ascensionis*
	Cleaning Goby	*Gobiosoma genie*
84.	Diamond Blenny	*Malacoctenus boehlkei*
	Sea Anemone	*Condylactis gigantea* (Weinland)
85.	Red Hind	*Epinephelus guttatus*
86.	Flower Coral	*Eusmilia fastigiata* (Pallas)
87.	Christmas Hydroid	*Sertularella speciosa* Congdon
88.	Reef Squid	*Sepioteuthis sepioidea* (Blainville)